The Art Quilt

QUILT VISIONS
2006

An Exhibition of Forty-Three Quilts

Edited by Patti Sevier

QUILT SAN DIEGO / QUILT VISIONS

ACKNOWLEDGEMENTS

The collective vision of many individuals has made this, the ninth biennial juried international exhibition of Quilt San Diego/Quilt Visions, possible. I extend my gratitude and appreciation to the following individuals:
Members of the Board of Directors of Quilt San Diego/Quilt Visions:
Charlotte Bird, Kathleen McCabe, Robbin Neff, Phyllis Newton,
Sue Robertson, Janice Taylor

Jurors for **Quilt Visions 2006 -***The Art Quilt*:
Jane Dunnewold, Lloyd Herman, Patricia Malarcher
Photographer: Mike Campos of Campos Photography
CD Production: Philip Bond of PME Audio/Visual
Technical Assistance: Ben Sevier

We are grateful to our partner in the production of this exhibit, the beautiful Oceanside Museum of Art. The following individuals at OMA have provided invaluable assistance during all phases of the production of **Quilt Visions 2006 -***The Art Quilt*: James R. Pahl, Beth Smith and Catherine Gleason.

Copy editing: Charlotte Bird, Leesa Zarinelli Gawlik, Miriam Machell, Tina Fellows, Patricia Klem, Jill Le Croissette

Patti Sevier
President, Board of Directors
Quilt San Diego/Quilt Visions

A Visions Publication
PMB# 372
12463 Rancho Bernardo Road
San Diego, CA 92128-2143

Cover Art - *The Light of Day* by Patty Hawkins

Library of Congress Cataloging-in-Publication Data
LC # 2006931710
ISBN - 09724664-2-8
Printed in China through Global Interprint

OCEANSIDE MUSEUM OF ART

DIRECTOR'S STATEMENT

Oceanside Museum of Art proudly presents its third Quilt Visions exhibition, **Quilt Visions 2006 - *The Art Quilt*.** Continuing its tradition of presenting art quilts from around the world, this show was organized by Quilt San Diego/Quilt Visions. A distinguished panel of jurors selected the show from 725 entries submitted by 318 artists from 20 countries. As one of the most prestigious art quilt exhibitions of international scope, it is especially exciting this year to feature the work of 16 artists who are appearing in a Quilt Visions exhibition for the first time. The consistency of these biennial productions has guaranteed that this documentary publication, when combined with the catalogs of past Quilt Visions exhibits, becomes a richly illustrated history of the quilt-maker's art as it has evolved throughout the last two decades.

Once again, the thoroughly professional Quilt Visions team has provided endless time and energy to make this project possible. Patti Sevier, Quilt San Diego President, spearheaded the effort together with Vice President Charlotte Bird. I wish to thank them and the other members of the Quilt San Diego/Quilt Visions board for both their hard work and dedication to this elegant art form. Special thanks also go to jurors Jane Dunnewold, Patricia Malarcher, and Lloyd Herman for accepting the difficult challenge of selecting 43 works of art from a field of exceptional quality.

I am grateful to Irv and Valya Simpson for organizing this year's jury theater, and to Catherine Gleason, OMA Director of Exhibitions and Collections, for her sensitive gallery design and careful installation of the exhibit.

The OMA docents and Quilt San Diego docents have joined together to lend their knowledge and insight into one of contemporary art's most expressive media. They provide tours for groups and casual drop-ins, sharing their enthusiasm for the quilts and the artists who create them. I hope all who visit the museum will spend time with these informative educators.

James R. Pahl

Executive Director

3

CRITERIA FOR SELECTION

The vision of Quilt Visions 2006 is that art quilting is and should be treated as a fine art, just as painting and sculpture. Artistic expression is universal, and the criteria for judging it should vary only as techniques of execution and inherent esthetics of medium necessarily vary with the materials of the art. Specific goals for our jurors, as scholarly art critics, are to select work for this show that reflects the universality of artistic expression and to report in their comments on how this show displays art quilting in the broader contemporary art context.

JANE DUNNEWOLD

Vital movements require a healthy mix of mature professionals and eager, creative newcomers. The 2006 Visions exhibition demonstrates this vitality. A number of participants have been included in this exhibition at least once in the past and in some cases, many more times than once. The newcomers who were selected are exploring fresh ideas and infusing the art quilt world with bursts of important energy.

When we sat down to review slides, I hoped the three of us would be able to choose as many new, deserving works as possible. Because we were selecting 43 pieces from a field of more than 700, I wanted our selections to be the finest examples of art quilts shown today. I hoped we would make discoveries that would thrill us. Perhaps what I observed isn't surprising, but it IS worth sharing.

There is a reason the same artists are shown year after year after year, and it is not the prejudice or whim of the jurors. Great artists are dedicated to their medium, to refining craft, and to perfecting technique and it shows. Mature works are strong visually and demonstrate the aspects of thoughtful composition and color treatment that contribute to successful work. When there is a theme, it is coherent. Maybe not right in your face. Subtlety is good. Too many beginners believe they have to tell the whole story.... A mature artist knows where to draw the line and doesn't give the whole story away, trusting the audience to discover the story for itself.

A dilemma arose as we compared notes on the various entries. When is generating a style/theme/colorway repeatedly, a "one trick pony", and when is it the thoughtful development of a mature body of work? It goes without saying that some artists' works have been shown so often they are instantly recognizable. How does a jury handle that recognition fairly? It's a knotty problem. The answer cycled back to the integrity of the work being viewed and its demonstration of development beyond what might have been seen last year....in effect, the artist's attention to continued refinement of craft. Well made pieces DO stand out when all is said and done.

BUT I had to admire artists who have made a conscious choice to explore new techniques, especially when it means developing a whole new approach to working. Several of the pieces included in this show, like Liz Axford's *Surface Tension* represent a major shift for an established artist. Other artists whose work is shifting may not have been included this time, but it isn't because the shift wasn't worth making. Rather, the work may still be incubating and may not be resolved yet. This is a state of discomfort many of us recognize and anyone who is experiencing it should be applauded for taking risks. I'll look forward to the inclusion of those new pieces next time around.

When newcomers were included, it was because the work was effectively composed, exhibited an effective use of color, and/or told a story that delighted and engaged us. We were particularly impressed when an entire set of entries succeeded, as did the work submitted by Marianne Burr. Three strong pieces is an indication of discipline and commitment on the part of the artist, and that is what it takes to become an artist whose work is chosen over and over again for competitions like Quilt Visions.

Jane Dunnewold

Jane Dunnewold, the author of three books, <u>Complex Cloth: A Comprehensive Guide to Surface Design</u>, <u>15 Beads: A Guide to Creating One-Of-a-Kind Beads</u>, and <u>Improvisational Screen Printing</u>, specializes in the creation of art cloth, one-of-a-kind lengths of printed fabric. She chaired the Surface Design Studio at the Southwest School of Art and Craft for eleven years and opened a private teaching space, Art Cloth Studios, in 2000. In 2000, a length of her art cloth won the Gold prize at the Taegu, Korea International Textile Exhibition. Her work has been exhibited in numerous invitational and juried exhibitions, including Quilt National (2000, 1997, 1995, and 1993), and Quilt Visions San Diego (2002, 1997, 1995) where her quilt, *Two Sides to Every Story* won the Quilt Japan Prize. Dunnewold produces more than 100 one-of-a-kind lengths of fabric every year.
Jane Dunnewold maintains an extensive teaching schedule at Art Cloth Studios in San Antonio, Texas where she lives with her daughter, Zenna, and numerous cats and dogs.

LLOYD HERMAN

Quilts have been cherished in American families for centuries; holding memories, they warmed our beds before they were deemed too beautiful to risk wearing out. The accepted history of the quilt is the sewing together of memories—worn-out clothes recycled with creativity and skill into colorful bed covers. Quilts—old and new—are our most enduring, and endearing, traditional art and continue to enthrall museum visitors.

The idea of the "art quilt" is only about thirty years old. I remember the first time that a major American art museum recognized the artistry of nineteenth century women who had no academic art training, but who made pieced quilts that art curators saw as the near-equivalent of abstract and color-field paintings. It was at the Whitney Museum of American Art in New York and, soon after we opened the Smithsonian Institution's Renwick Gallery in 1972, we also exhibited those quilts from the collection of Jonathan Holstein and Gail van der Hoof.

"The Artist and the Quilt" exhibition and book in 1983, brought together quilt makers with painters to "collaborate" on stitched and stuffed fabric works that were shown nationally in museums. But they weren't really collaborations at all; for the most part, quilters were asked to take the imagery of the painters and recreate it in fabric. I'm guessing that quilt makers across the country bristled that their own ideas weren't good enough to stand on their own, and resolved to break free of the restrictions of the pieced block quilt or crazy quilt to find their own styles in quilt art.

Though this all happened several decades ago, the time was already ripe with new possibilities for embellishing the fabric surface. Textile specialists were already examining the creative possibilities in the Asian textile dyeing and patterning techniques that had been introduced to them in the 1960s—*batik, itak* and *plangi* for example—and finding fresh new ways to use them. Coupled with a renewed interest in embroidery and beadwork, as well as direct dyeing, drawing and painting on fabric, their efforts framed the new surface design movement.

Though I know a little bit about textile techniques, I was the "generalist" on this panel of selectors—a craft specialist who sees creative expression in wood, fiber, metal, glass and clay in the larger context of American visual art history. Yes, I have curated exhibitions that included quilts and other art fabrics, and have juried national and international textile competitions. But my knowledge of this field is not so deep that I can always recognize the process used by an artist, or evaluate the deftness of its use—or name its maker when seeing a distinctive style.

Though the convention of the repeated block composition is still present in today's art quilts, more often than not artists are breaking totally free of tradition. In this competition there were still circle-in-square repeats that recall the "Rocky Road to Dublin" or "Drunkard's Path" pattern, but different. Strip-pieced quilts hardly resembled "Log Cabin" variations. In fact, it almost seemed like a new "tradition" to create horizontal bands of narrow, vertical strips. Likewise, we saw numerous examples of these two types that juxtaposed light and dark fabrics, or those with reverberating color, to create optical effects. Geometric compositions often were not repeats, but large rectangles overlaid with smaller ones, sometimes made with sheer fabrics for a veiled effect. I had to ask my two fellow fabric artist jurors, who work fulltime in textiles as teacher and journalist as well, to tell me if styles we saw again and again were the hallmark of a particular teacher or trend.

Just as some of the eye-popping optical effects may take "fine arts" inspiration from the Op Art movement, or recall layers of imagery familiar in Robert Rauschenberg's prints and paintings, others referred to figurative painting and drawing, including historical art. We chose examples that showed a sure sense of composition and originality. Others, however, brought us to a discussion of the need for artists who choose a representational style in any medium to master realistic drawing, and then to employ it with an original viewpoint.

These discussions raise the question of what makes an "art" quilt, but I began to ponder just what it is that makes a quilt. Sandwiches of fabric stitched together? One or two of the works we chose had little more than a stitched line or two; others were almost entirely embroidered. It all seemed a far cry from discussions nearly twenty-five years ago when I served on the jury for Quilt National. Major concerns then were whether entries were hand or machine quilted! And the number of quilting stitches per square inch is not even a factor today; I was more concerned that the workmanship exhibited was appropriate to the precision, or looseness, of the artist's apparent intent.

Clearly, the art quilt has come a long way in the last three decades, and it will continue to evolve. Heat transfer of photographic images has given way to direct digital printing of fabric, and the traditional calico and gingham—indeed most commercial patterned fabrics—have been superseded by artist-embellished materials.

I applaud Quilt San Diego for launching, and continuing, this important international competition, and for inviting me to participate in the selection of the 2006 exhibition. And, as the organization prepares to move into a new, permanent exhibition facility in San Diego, I will stand and cheer this increasingly vigorous avenue of creative expression.

Lloyd E. Herman

Lloyd Herman has been a recognized observer of America's contemporary craft movement for thirty-five years. He was founding Director of the Renwick Gallery of the Smithsonian Institution from 1971 until 1986. Later he directed the Cartwright Gallery in Vancouver, British Columbia and supervised its evolution into the Canadian Craft Museum.

Mr. Herman has lectured on American crafts throughout the United States and abroad. He has juried numerous art competitions and curated such traveling exhibitions as "Trashformations: Recycled Materials in American Art and Design," and "American Glass: Masters of the Art." He has written several books on American craft including Art That Works: The Decorative Arts of the Eighties, Crafted in America. He has hosted television programs on contemporary craft in Canada and has produced and narrated an award-winning video on five American glass artists.

He is a member of the international advisory boards of the International Tapestry Network (ITNET), Arango Design Foundation, Friends of Fiber Art International and The Crafts Center, Washington, D.C. He is an honorary Fellow of the American Craft Council. He serves on the board of the Arrowmont School of Arts and Crafts. He is a native of Oregon who lives and works in Seattle, Washington

PATRICIA MALARCHER

It was a pleasure and a challenge to watch the projected procession of hundreds of slides from which approximately 40 pieces, less than ten per cent, could be chosen for Quilt Visions 2006. Assuredly, this array proclaimed the state of the art of the art quilt today.

Observations made early on in the art quilt movement are now assumptions. Many years ago, Penny McMorris, writing in the book that accompanied the exhibition, The Art Quilt,* noted distinctions between the art quilt and the quilt for the bed. Among them was the art quilt's rise from the horizontal bed to the art-privileged wall. Thus the art quilt exists as a hybrid that combines the 2D space of painting with its identity as pliable fabric.

As jurors, we reviewed how this combination is being realized 20 years after The Art Quilt's first publication. Is it telling that, during the first round of jurying, following an overview of all the submissions, there were numerous "Nos," a handful of resonant "Yesses," and an enormous middle ground of "Maybes?" Were we just being cautious about commitment or had the works arrived at a certain plateau where many are good but few are outstanding?

Differences became more apparent as we fine-tuned our choices over several viewings. The selection process was also an effort to represent diverse directions the movement has taken. Inevitably, the question, "Is that a quilt?" arose and provoked discussion, especially in cases where painterly images seemed more dominant than quilterly character.

While there were fresh, innovative uses of commercially printed fabric, it was clear that a critical mass of artists are dyeing, painting, printing, stitching, embellishing, and manipulating fabric surfaces to satisfy their artistic intentions. This year, discharge (the removal of color from fabric) seemed especially prevalent. With inkjet printing added to their toolboxes, many artists are incorporating images from endless resources—e.g., original photographs, newspapers, art historical archives.

In preparation for these remarks, I sought perspective on how this show would depart from its predecessors. Browsing through quilt books and catalogs from the past decade, I concluded that, due to available technology, a dramatic increase of photographic images is a sign of the time.

Re-examining the "Quilt Visions 2004" catalog— I had only glanced at it earlier, wanting to concentrate on the 2006 entries—I saw that many artists whose work we had picked were represented by similar pieces in the previous show. However, other artists, whose quilts we did not select, were also represented by pieces that were not very different from those we viewed. (This should encourage artists to re-enter shows, since each jury brings three new pairs of eyes.)

This recurrence of similar images prompts me to play the devil's advocate, asking about the pace of change in the art quilt field as compared with that in the larger art world. It seems that art quilt surface designers move ahead collectively, assimilating new techniques as they are disseminated through the community. Thus, despite a wide range of subjects and styles—e.g., abstract, geometric, figurative, landscape, narrative, still life, portraiture—quilt shows tend to have a homogeneous flavor.

Although fabric can reach out in any direction, most artists—a couple of exceptions this year moved their work from the wall to the pedestal—adhere to a rectangular format. Few seem to be investigating the meaning of the quilt as a flexible object as well as a surface. Are there unexplored expressive possibilities in overall shape? Another consideration: Quilts now tend to be close to the size of domestic paintings and prints while the large scale of traditional historical quilts was part of their visual impact.

Is the essence of the quilt its materiality, the "fabric sandwich," or is it, like a vessel, an archetypal form with connotations that relate to human experience? Might artists find inspiration in revisiting its functional origins? For example, might the quilt be interpreted in terms of our neo-nomadic lifestyle, in which our worlds are contained within hand-held devices?

All this leads me to wonder where to look for the cutting edge of quiltdom. Is it within the fiber art realm or is it in the fine art world where artists claim to be driven by concepts rather than process and materials?

As questions emerge, I am grateful to the Quilt Visions organizers who assembled the works that engaged my eyes and provoked me to think. Hopefully, Quilt Visions 2006 not only will be a beautiful show, but also will stimulate viewers to ponder over the nature of quiltness and its contribution to the universe of art.

*Penny McMorris and Michael Kyle, The Art Quilt, Quilt Digest Press, 1996.

Patricia Malarcher

Patricia Malarcher is a studio artist as well as the Editor of the Surface Design Journal and Surface Design Association Newsletter. She has contributed chapters to books including Objects and Meaning (Scarecrow Press), Helena Hernmarck: Tapestry Artist (Byggforlaget), and Michael James: Art & Inspiration (C&T Publishing). She has written essays for exhibition catalogs including Generations/Transformations (American Textile History Museum), Cultures Revealed: Appliques from Around the World (Visual Arts Center, North Carolina State University/Raleigh), and Threads: Fiber in the '90s (New Jersey Center for Visual Arts).

Ms. Malarcher was a recipient of a James Renwick Fellowship for research in craft criticism. Her pieced constructions have been shown internationally and are in many public and private collections. She lives and works in Englewood, New Jersey.

SPONSORS

The fiber artist of today owes much to the many wonderful people and companies that provided the tools and materials used to create the works of art presented in this exhibit. Without the efforts of fabric manufacturers, quilt shops, guilds, artists, galleries and collectors, fiber art as we know and enjoy it would not be possible. Quilt Visions acknowledges and commends our valued sponsors for their many contributions to the arts in general and this exhibition in particular.

ROSIE GONZALEZ
Rosie's Calico Cupboard

We acknowledge Rosie Gonzalez, owner of Rosie's Calico Cupboard Quilt Shop, as a benefactor and true friend to this exhibition. We are especially grateful for her unfailing support during the last twelve years.

Rowenta
Friends of Fiber Arts International
Cozy Quilt Shop

La Jolla FiberArts Gallery
Margrette Carr
First National Bank
Glendale Quilt Guild

Michael Miller Fabrics
E. E. Schenck Company

Friendship Quilt Guild
Beach Cities Quilters Guild
El Camino Quilters
Island Batik, Inc.
P&B Fabrics
Red Rooster Fabrics
Starseed Foundation
C & T Publishing

AWARDS

The **Quilts Japan Prize,** is sponsored by Nihon Vogue Company, LDT. The jurors selected Patty Hawkins, Estes Park, Colorado, to receive this award for her work *The Light of Day*. The objective of the Quilts Japan Prize is to express gratitude for the continued growth of the Japanese quilt, which is due in great part to American quilters, and to pay respect to the predecessors of quiltmaking. With this award, Nihon Vogue hopes to play a role in the development of quiltmaking by helping to link the ties between Japanese and American quiltmakers.

The **Sponsor's Award** is given by Rosie Gonzalez of Rosie's Calico Cupboard Quilt Shop who selected *Primitive Door Series #30 Haunted House* by Vita Marie Lovett, Maryville, Tennessee. "As soon as I saw this quilt, I knew it was the one that I would end up choosing. I love the detail of the lace curtain and you just wait to walk through that door to see what's on the other side. Simple but most effective."

The **La Jolla FiberArts Award** is given by Lynn Noble owner of La Jolla FiberArts Gallery to Marianne Burr from Coopeville, Washington for her work *Frank's Melons*. The award is an acknowledgement of artistic ability and is intended to encourage fiber artists to explore more fully the medium of the art quilt.

The **CREAM Award**, (Cathy Rasmussen Emerging Artist Memorial Award) is awarded by the Studio Art Quilt Association to an artist with a work in a Quilt Visions exhibition for the first time. The CREAM Award is so named in memory of SAQA's first executive director, Cathy Rasmussen. The board of directors of SAQA have chosen Joan Sowada of Gillette, Wyoming as the recipient of this year's award for her work *Cosmic Bicycle*.

The **Brakensiek "Caught Our Eye" Award** is presented to Katie Pasquini Masopust of Santa Fe, New Mexico for her piece, *Legerrio*. Nancy and Warren Brakensiek are longtime contemporary art quilt collectors living in Albuquerque, New Mexico. Their collection consists of over 140 art quilts. They believe that a collector's eye can be different from that of professional judges or experts.

The **President's Choice Award**, given by Glendale Quilt Guild, is chosen by the President of Quilt San Diego/Quilt Visions. Patti Sevier has selected *Return* by Elizabeth Busch of Glenburn, Maine.

The jurors selected *Curtain Call for Aphrodite* by Lori Lupe Pelish, Niskayuna, New York for the **Friends of Fiber Arts International Award** as the quilt which most reflects the universality of artistic expression.

The **Surface Design Award** is presented for work which exemplifies the Surface Design Association's mission to inspire, encourage and further the rich tradition of the textile arts through the creative exploration of coloring, patterning and structuring of fiber and fabric. It is presented to Judy Langille, Glen Ridge, New Jersey for *Striped Formations*.

Title	Artist
Surface Tension	Liz Axford
Rainy Rainy Night	Elizabeth Barton
Frank's Melons	Marianne Burr
Return	Elizabeth Busch
Sending Up Prayers	Jette Clover
In Winter Woods	Linda Colsh
Las Mañanitas	Karen Cunagin
Minutia #4	Martha Bruin Degen
Conical Rhythm	Joan Lockburner Deuel
Silent Sentinels	Noriko Endo
Rock Fissures	Pamela Fitzsimons
Eat Your Veggies	Laura Fogg
Net 8	Ruth Garrison
Waiting for the Rain	Margery Goodall
Time Is As Weak As Water	Carol Anne Grotrian
The Light of Day	Patty Hawkins
Sea Form	Wendy Hill
From 23rd St. to 70th St.	Harumi Iida
Striped Formations	Judy Langille
Intrusion	Robert S. Leathers
Primitive Door Series #30 - Haunted House	Vita Marie Lovett
Trees, Lumber, Houses, People	Linda MacDonald
Legerrio	Katie Pasquini Masopust
Multiple Perspectives	Patricia Mink
Secret Diary 19:"more, faster, hurry up!"	Angela Moll
Well-Handled Cloth	Anne McKenzie Nickolson
Stir It Up	Dan Olfe
Curtain Call for Aphrodite	Lori Lupe Pelish
Abstraction in Blue with a Red Line	Julia E. Pfaff
Mysterious Migration of Miscellaneous Objects	Pam RuBert
Fledgling	Dinah Sargeant
Pillars	Joan Schulze
Katrina Blues	Susan Shie
All in the Family	Mary Ruth Smith
Heart's Desire: Magma Rising	Karen N. Soma
Cosmic Bicycle	Joan Sowada
Deschutes #1	Connie Tiegel
#45 Big Head Series - The Dancer	Kristin Tweed
Palms Swaying, Whales Breeching	Nelda Warkentin
Tree Series #2: Canadian Sunrise	Barbara W. Watler
Cyborg Female 4: Mother Wit	Kathy Weaver
Tangled	Jill Rumoshosky Werner
In a Different Vein	Elia Woods

THE QUILTS

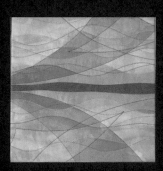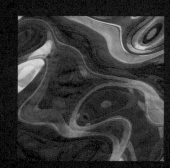

Liz Axford

Houston, Texas

USA

Since 2002, I have been exploring alternate ways to create textiles sharing structural characteristics with quilts – three layers, with stitching penetrating all layers – but of less graphic, less rigid, and more nuanced effect. I now substitute dyed and printed silk organza for the cotton quilt top and backing, and visible handmade wool felt for the unseen cotton batting. The three layers are laminated together in the felting process.

Surface Tension is the third in my series of Log Jam quilts. Intended to be seen from both sides, it juxtaposes log shapes with wave shapes, and is designed such that log shapes on the front are backed with wave shapes, and vice versa. Once stitched from both sides, the relationship between the two different systems of patterning, logs and waves, becomes evident.

53 x 30 inches

Silk organza, wool roving, cotton embroidery floss.

Screen printing with thickened dyes, immersion dyeing, felting, stitching.

Front

Back

Elizabeth Barton

Athens, Georgia
USA

Since Spring of 2005, I've been working on a series of quilts about the myths of Drowned Cities. I was fascinated by the idea of cities under water – the old myths about Atlantis and Is (in Brittany), Semmerwater in England and Debussy's Cathedrale Engloutie and many others. Even Harry Potter encounters a drowned city in one of his adventures! There is a sense of beauty and elegance, of tarnished memories and mystery, but also retribution from a thwarted Nature that weaves a complex pattern of serenity and watchful threat. These ideas were all too prophetic as I saw with the effects of hurricanes upon New Orleans last Fall.

Rainy Rainy Night is one of my favorites from the series – it tells the story of the continuing promise of comforting warmth from the windows of the houses despite the siege of the water.

35 x 59 inches

Cotton fabric hand dyed or discharged, shibori.

Pieced and appliqued and quilted by machine.

Marianne Burr

Coupeville, Washington
USA

I got seriously interested in fruits and vegetables when the news came of my 293 cholesterol level. Where could that have come from? Better yet, where is it going? I keep going to farmers' markets and the produce there is more than good to eat. It's good to look at and sketch. Hello fruit cup, hello art!

49 x 38 inches

10mm silk, merino wool felt, cotton, hand dyed silk and cotton threads, woven ribbon.

Silk painting, block printing, hand and machine quilting, hand applique.

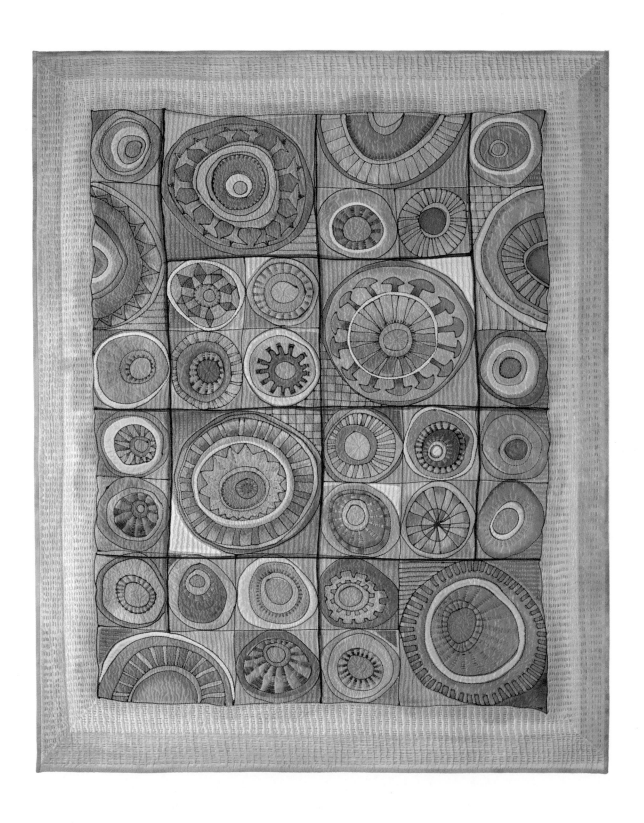

Elizabeth Busch

Glenburn, Maine
USA

In 2001, I began painting on black fabric. Using both textile paints and acrylics, the pieces reflect the results of my ongoing exploration of this process. In *Return*, the fabric inherently creates infinite space which allows me to build layer upon layer in both opaque and translucent forms. My work is about layering and spatial illusion, whether I am using transparent colors on raw cotton canvas, theater gels in my hanging sculptures, or black fabric as you see here. Listen to the sound, feel the temperature.

40 x 20 inches

Fabric, paint, embroidery floss, poly batt, cotton back.

Air brush, drawing, machine piecing, hand quilting.

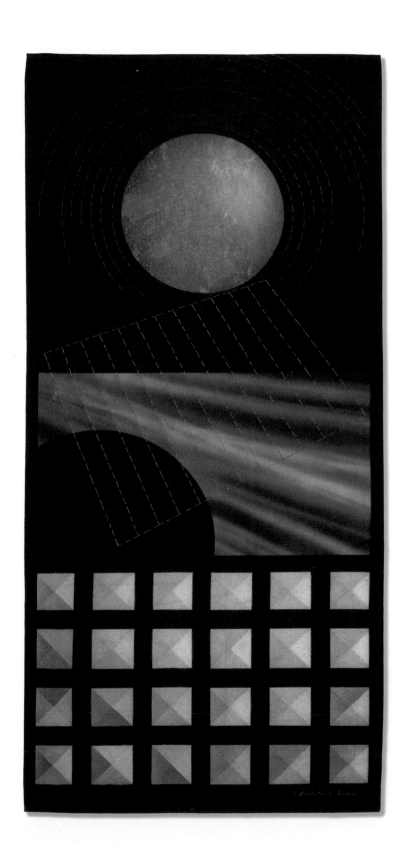

Jette Clover

Antwerpen

Belgium

When my dog died I started to explore all the possibilities of black and white through the discharge technique. I grew very fond of all the shades of grey, and it became a challenge to change the mood by adding an accent color.

40 x 51 inches

Cotton, silk, cheese cloth discharge.

Hand dyed, collage, hand and machine quilting.

Linda Colsh

Everberg

Belgium

The Omega Woman is alone, silent, and everywhere. She exists in fog: unseen, unheard, ignored. But she is an army.

In a series of art quilts featuring the Omega Woman, I want to examine those aspects of what most likely will become of us all as we age and as there are more of the "old us."

68 x 48 inches

Cotton fabrics: dyed, discharged, and printed by the artist.

Machine pieced and machine quilted, computer images and screen printing by the artist.

Karen Cunagin
Fallbrook, California
USA

My work is visual storytelling - rehearsing the people, events, and causes I value.

This original design commemorates a spiritual retreat experience of Las Mañanitas--the Spanish custom of celebrating a birthday--being showered with music and masses of flowers.

I am a passionate quilter, dumbstruck by this enormous love--soaked in the music of the spheres' vast, eternal melodies and laden with more blossoms than I can possibly carry. Receiving fresh vision, this inspires my continuing body of work.

56 x 49 inches

Cotton, silk, paper, beads, embroidery floss.

Traditional machine piecing, soft-edge machine applique, hand-sewn, -beaded and -applied yo-yos, quilted with 20-year-old Singer machine, computer-printed text on paper, fabric ink-enhanced coloration.

Martha Bruin Degan

Staunton, Virginia
USA

Current events, as reflected through social and political behaviors, and the dynamics of personal and family relationships interest me and are featured in my art. My goal is to communicate the questions and encourage the viewer to address the questions that arise from these themes, rather than make pronouncements about them. I have found that people are drawn to the inherently warm and non-threatening qualities of fabric and quilts, which encourages them to confront topics that they may otherwise prefer to avoid.

The juxtaposition of the various shapes, textures, color, and patterns of fabric pieces is as deliberate and purposeful as drawing with charcoal or painting with a brush. I liken the process of assembling and stitching the layers of an art quilt to drawing with thread, creating images that become metaphorical expressions of life and our interaction with others.

48 x 43 inches

Found objects, textile paint and ink, rayon, cotton, plastic, markers, pastels.

Hand and machine assembled/quilted, drawn and painted images.

Joan Lockburner Deuel
Richford, New York
USA

Contemplating the flexible nature of quilted textiles
and my interest in lines quilted and other, it seems
natural to me to flex the quilt and move the line away
from the wall.

Lines and color, how they relate to each other,
moving from simple to complex, are elements that
I have observed all my life. Growth lines from
wood grain, fungus and leaves reflect the line
that came before and the conditions of the present
growing season. These lines become an ebb and flow
movement and rhythm that is almost musical.

53 x 71 inches

Dye painted cotton broadcloth, canvas,
cotton batting, velcro, polyneon thread.

Dye painting, shibori, machine pieced,
machine quilted.

Noriko Endo
Narashino, Chiba
Japan

This piece is part of a recent series of work that deals with landscapes. While walking in a dark beech forest, I have discovered a place of mystery and wonder. I felt nature kept some of her hidden secrets. I am totally absorbed and fascinated by the beauty of nature. Beech woods were chased by the light.

66 x 76 inches

Hand-dyed cotton, tulle, metallic thread, small pieces covered with tulle.

Machine quilted, appliqued, machine embellished.

Pamela Fitzsimons

Mount Vincent, New South Wales
Australia

The Australian landscape is vast and overwhelming, shaped and marked by time and the elements; this is my 'home place' and my inspiration. I am interested in exploring concepts of place and time and use 'slow' techniques to convey my ideas. In this piece wool has been dyed with eucalyptus leaves, collaged together and hand stitched.

34 x 30 inches

Plant dyed wool, wool batting, silk backing.

Appliqued and hand stitched with silk and rayon threads.

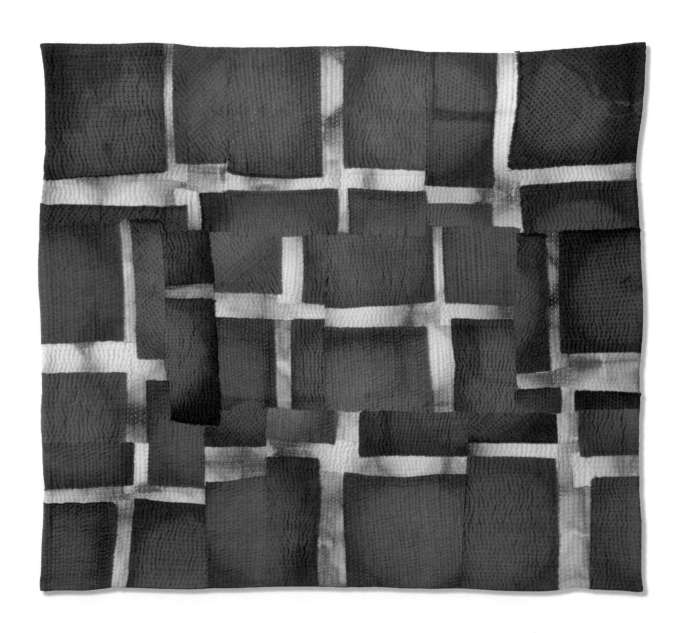

Laura Fogg
Ukiah, California
USA

This irregularly shaped quilt depicts a huge table laden with home cooked veggie dishes of all descriptions. All are displayed on fanciful plates, trays or baskets, and most are embellished with herbs and serving implements. Behind the table is me, sporting a culinary apron, and behind me is my kitchen window and the artifacts that reside there, including the kitchen witch and spider plant. Through the window is the view out into my vegetable garden.

91 x 89 inches

Commercial cotton prints, upholstery fabric, metallics, napkins, antique doilies, knit fabric, tulle, raffia, transparent ribbon, Sulky rayon quilting thread.

Raw-edge machine applique, machine quilting, machine embroidery on Solvy, machine satin stitch applique.

Ruth Garrison
Flagstaff, Arizona
USA

In my Net series of quilts I have chosen to explore certain formal elements of design within a limited color range. These include the interaction of shape and line, the contrast of values, subtle variations in color, and the many ways in which a rectangular plane can be divided into zones of pattern and color.

39 x 61 inches

Artist dyed cotton fabrics, cotton batting, cotton thread.

Hand dyeing, machine piecing, machine quilting.

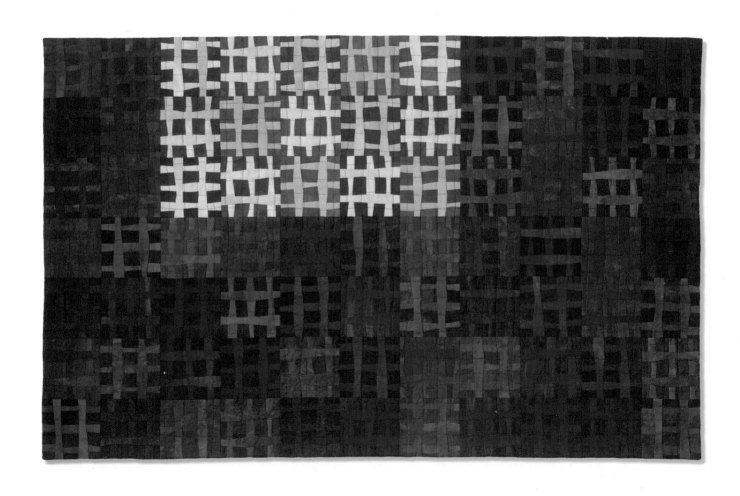

Margery Goodall

Mount Lawley, Western Australia
Australia

My focus is to create rhythm using line, space and colour. I work constantly at simplifying – taking what I see, re-shaping and communicating.

I make stitched textiles to express my ideas about living in Australia. *Waiting for the Rain* is one of several quilts which look at landscape. In this arid environment and harsh climate, even with the best of methods, conventional farming in Australia takes a leap of faith. Farmers and their families deal with uncertainty on a daily basis – fragile soils and drought are always there. When will the rain come?

48 x 48 inches

Fabrics: hand-printed cotton, commercial cotton and cotton blends, silk, rayon, textile printing inks and dyes.

Machine stitched, hand printing, dye painting.

Carol Anne Grotrian

Cambridge, Massachusetts

USA

Various shibori techniques and indigo dye create the
organic patterns that bring this shore to life, where
even solid rocks are worn away by the persistent
power of water over time. Time plays another role,
since the image of these rocks on a friend's beach
hovered in the back of my mind for years before
materializing in a quilt. It is these lasting, back
burner images that often provide the strongest
content in my work. The title is taken from a song by
Brazilian Caetano Veloso.

30 x 35 inches

Indigo-dyed shibori cotton.

Indigo dyeing, many shibori techniques,
pieced and quilted by hand and machine.

Patty Hawkins
Estes Park, Colorado
USA

The white bark and dark elk scarring of aspen trees, consistently beckon me to creat abstracted groves of aspen; my artist residency in Rocky Mountain National Park enhances this motivation.

I use net overlays to suggest the bare branches of winter. These skeletal trees give ME a quiet beauty; contrasting the attraction to most of Colorado's golden aspen fall. The tree imagery offers me comfort, stability, solitude, tranquility, longevity; aspiring human qualities.

Shibori dyeing, to create my aspen bark fabric, is done by scrunching fabric tightly on a tube: a Japanese technique. Deconstructed screen printing creates the "light of day" for the distance in this quilt. Appreciating the beauty of the scarred trees, equates to Wabi Sabi, the Japanese aesthetic which I espouse, honoring the beauty of simplicity and imperfection all around us.

39 x 84 inches

Artist hand-dyed fabrics, including shibori and silk-screening.

Machine pieced, overlay shapes of nylon netting, machine quilted.

Wendy Hill

Sunriver, Oregon
USA

Visual and physical textures are important to me, along with color, shape, and line. These elements play against each other in this convoluted piece – which can be playfully arranged and rearranged again and again. I like to surprise myself and the viewer.

The idea for this three dimensional, quilted flexible coil came to me after reading about a bias cut gown. Although I usually work with fabric in two dimensions, I often explore three dimensional forms in paper, other fibers, and fabric.

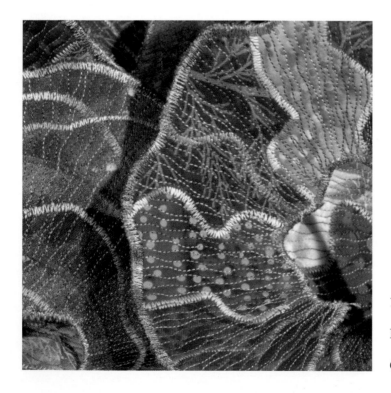

10 x 15 x 13 inches

Fabric, thread, fast2fuse.

Collage, thread texturing, quilting.

Sea Form

Harumi Iida
Kamakura

Japan

This is a memory of visiting New York in 2005. During one week, I stayed in a hotel on 23rd St. and visited museums, art galleries, city libraries, shops…. alone. The map of MTA helped me very much and became my best partner.

55 x 54 inches

Old Yukata fabrics (cotton), commercial fabrics (cotton).

Machine pieced, quilted, hand embroidered.

From 23rd St. to 70th St.

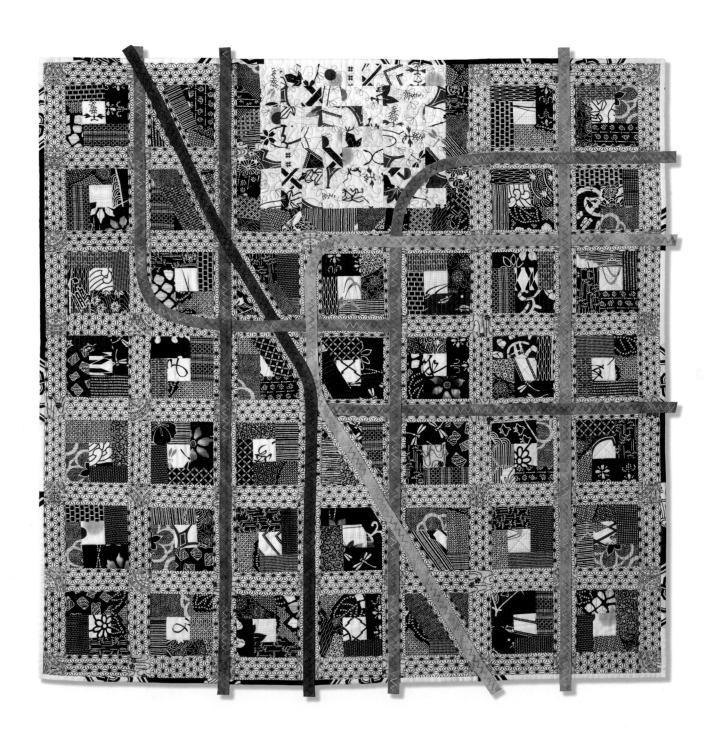

Judy Langille

Glen Ridge, New Jersey

USA

Striped Formations is part of a new series of quilts with which I have been experimenting. The basis for this series is the use of forms inspired by paper that is torn impulsively and in an unmeditated manner. I am interested in the spontaneity of the torn forms as well as the impromptu screening of color through a blank screen that creates the fabrics used in these pieces.

The torn paper is used as a resist and thickened dyes are screened on the fabric adding color. Many layers of dyes are added along with layers of discharge paste which removes some of the color and creates new shades. The fabrics are fused in order to create a design which reflects the improvisational formation of the fabrics into an ordered composition. Finally, the stitching creates a line that is drawn onto the surface of the fabric to bring the whole piece together.

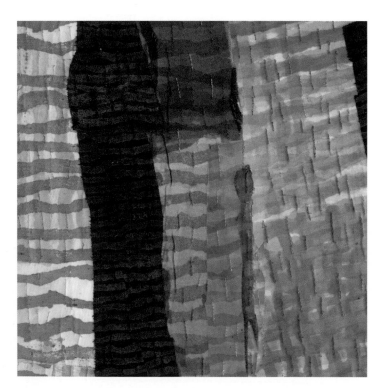

49 x 39 inches

Cotton, viscose challis, Procion MX thickened dyes, discharge paste, flannel, threads.

Torn paper resist with thick dyes and discharge paste screened through a blank screen, thermofax screen and hand painted, fused and machine stitched.

Robert S. Leathers
San Diego, California
USA

Intrusion is about manmade buildings and spaces invading the natural organic order. The struggle between architecture and nature occasionally results in an almost symbiotic relationship, but more frequently, is experienced in violent clashes. Unless we are sensitive to the environment we will have no future. Mankind intrudes on nature and nature fights back. This quilt is part of an ongoing series examining that struggle.

36 x 54 inches

Hand-dyed fabrics, photo-transferred cotton top, wool batting, cotton back, cotton thread, dye, paint and Prismacolor pencils.

Triple exposure in-camera, photo transfer to cotton, pieced, cotton thread stitchery.

Vita Marie Lovett

Maryville, Tennessee

USA

Legend has it that this seaside Victorian house is haunted. In the late 1800's Celeste Eppes, in an attempt to make her husband jealous, lied about his best friend having an interest in her. Her husband confronted him in the parlor of the house. He, of course, denied any wrongdoing but was shot with a bullet through his heart. The truth came out during the trial and the town shunned Celeste. She died a few years later during childbirth. She has been thought to have haunted this house ever since. People say you can see her peering out through the windows....

32 x 28 inches

Canvas, cotton, acrylic paint, cotton thread.

Painted canvas, machine thread painting throughout including lace curtain, machine quilted.

Primitive Door Series #30 - Haunted House

Linda MacDonald

Willits, California
USA

The timber industry in Northern California is still
a big part of the economy but is much diminished
as urban growth pushes out and our forests regrow
again and again. We need to continually assess and
monitor our natural resources.

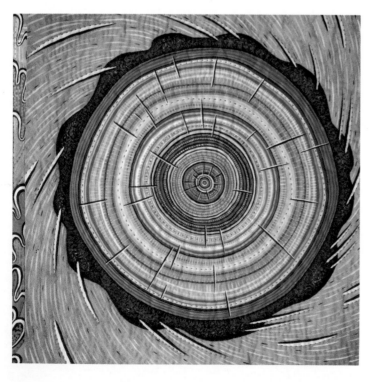

36 x 48 inches

Cottons, paints, threads.

Airbrushed surface, hand painting, hand
quilting.

Katie Pasquini Masopust

Santa Fe, New Mexico

USA

Legerrio is a musical term meaning light and airy.
This began as a small portion of a large painting.
I painted listening to light and airy music, greatly
enlarged and recreated in fabric.

78 x 81 inches

Cottons, blends and satin, wool batting.

Machine applique, machine quilted.

Patricia Mink

Johnson City, Tennessee
USA

My current work explores the traditional layered quilt form, employing new digital techniques for printing fabric, as a means of establishing a visual dialogue addressing issues of contemporary culture. Drawing from historic associations with domesticity, comfort, and home, the quilt form offers unique possibilities for developing content when combined with non-traditional techniques and unexpected imagery.

The images used in *Wall Quilt #31: Multiple Perspectives* are details from Leonardo da Vinci's "Last Supper," a very old fresco that has gone through much deterioration and many restorations over time. The half-glass images I've selected from the fresco work symbolically with the concept of perspective as outlook (1/2 full or empty?) as well as playing on the idea of 'Renaissance Perspective' (aka linear perspective and the idea of art as a window) and visual perception.

41 x 46 inches

Cotton muslin, pigmented inks, cotton and polyester thread, cotton batting, cotton backing.

Digitally manipulated reproduction of details from da Vinci's Last Supper, inkjet printed onto fabric, hand and machine stitched.

Angela Moll

Santa Barbara, California

USA

In the Secret Diary series I am looking inside, into the intimate space where journals are written, where quilts are stitched. The pages of my Secret Diaries are journal entries screen-printed on fabric. The text records the flow of thoughts as I write on the screen with dye. A quilted page is a layering of different screen printed entries, the superimposition of a day onto the next one. I use the collaged and stitched diary fragments to speak about intimacy, communication, as well as privacy and isolation. Each quilt is an open notebook, the oversized text an invitation to read. Yet the stitched diaries are unreadable, revealing just the outline of a life story: rhythm, pattern, layers. The pressure, intensity, and speed of the hand-written line imply the texture of emotions. It is an open book but a Secret Diary.

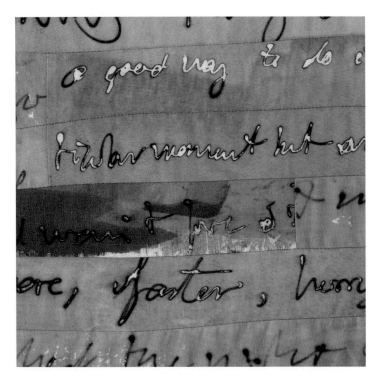

48 x 36 inches

Fiber reactive dye, cotton fabric.

Screenprinting, machine piecing and quilting.

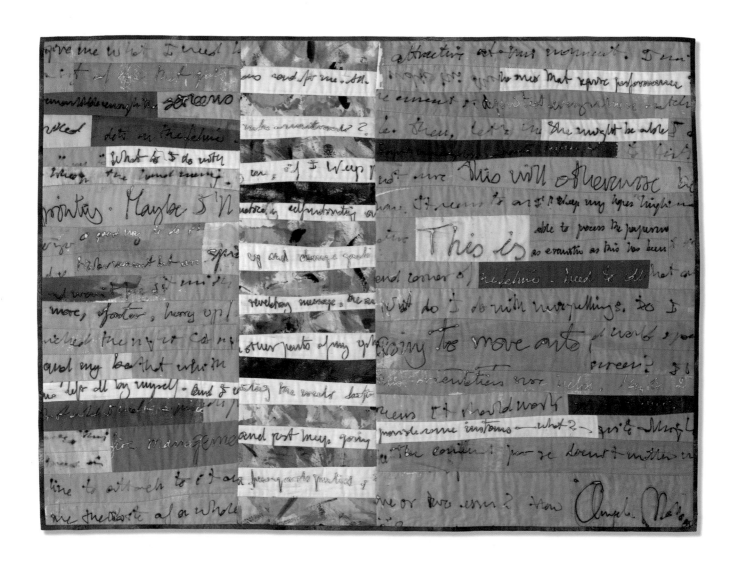

Anne McKenzie Nickolson

Indianapolis, Indiana

USA

My work has always explored my interest in
patterning with the creating of pictorial space.
Pattern is a distinctive feature of textiles and offers
rich possibilities for complex interaction of shape
and color. It is within this structure of pattern that I
like to introduce pictorial elements.

My current body of work uses images from the
world of painting and inserts these images into my
structured, layered textiles. *Well–Handled Cloth* is
based on one of the many versions of the legend of
St. Veronica. She is said to have wiped the dying
face of Christ and his image miraculously appeared
on her cloth. I find that cloth always bears witness
to those who have touched it. Cloth always connects
me to the maker or the loving user of the cloth and
as such, is evidence of a life.

47 x 47 inches

Cotton fabric, cotton batting.

Machine pieced, hand appliqued through
all layers, embroidery.

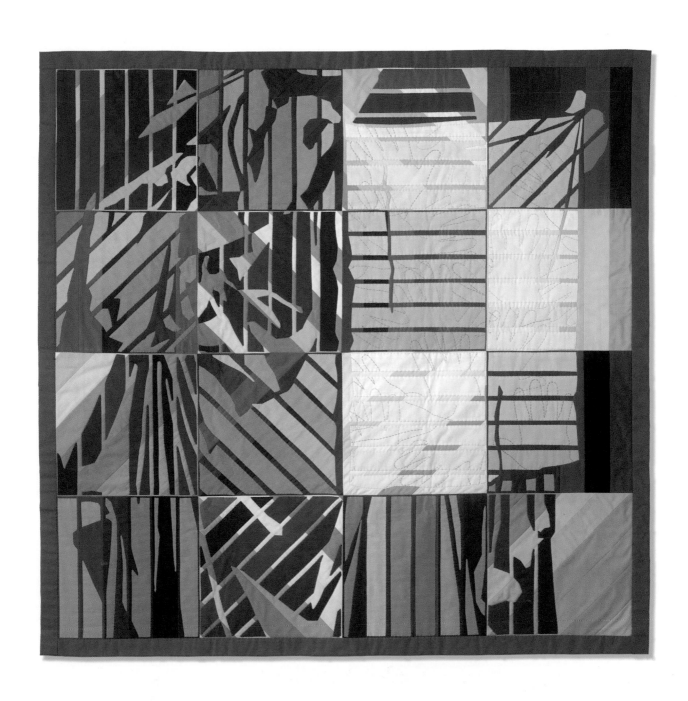

Dan Olfe
Julian, California
USA

I greatly enjoy working with color and transparency. To create the design for this quilt I used 3D software in two steps. First I created an image from a 3D computer scene in which light passed through a large number of colored glass pyramids. Then I "stirred up" the image of pyramids by viewing it through a simulated water surface. The final computer image was digitally printed on cloth and quilted as a whole-cloth quilt.

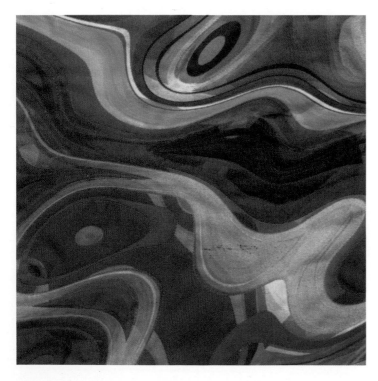

47 x 79 inches

Polyester whole cloth top, batting, cotton back, monofilament thread.

3D software was used to create the image, which was printed on cloth by a dye sublimation process.

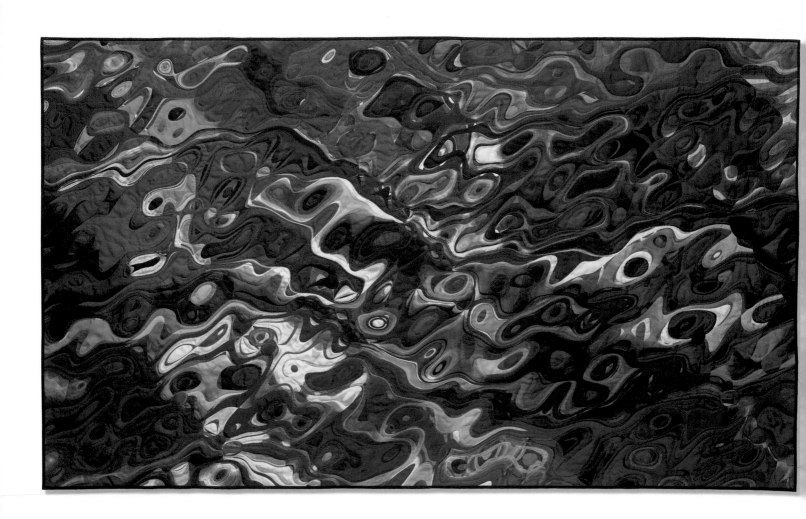

Lori Lupe Pelish

Niskayuna, New York
USA

A serene atmosphere of classical beauty is staged and presented, after waiting in the wings, ready to step out and make an appearance.

The bad news and tragic events of today can be terribly overwhelming. I constantly find myself being responsible to express and portray my feelings, which revolve around these events. But I also find myself grasping and clutching close to my heart the incredible beauty and goodness that subtly surround us all. The balancing of the tragic and the beautiful consumes.

Visually, beauty today can be harsh and aggressive, but the simple act of dressing for the prom in such an elegant way is what set the stage for this piece.

47 x 40 inches

Commercial cotton.

Machined appliqued, embroidered and quilted.

Julia E. Pfaff

Richmond, Virginia
USA

For several years my quilts have reflected my
involvement with archaeology. This quilt is part of
a series that returns to art for art sake. No exotic
artifacts, narratives, or allegories. This series
investigates the process of painting and this piece
represents the essence of abstraction. My interest
is the unique quality of dye on fabric and the way
marks are made on a two dimensional surface.

The final design is part accident and part controlled
application of dye and construction. My starting
point was a whole cloth used as a drop cloth while
I painted several narrow lengths of black fabric.
The design developed organically as I worked
further applying dye by hand. The final constructed
composition was then planned in response to the dye
painted forms.

51 x 42 inches

100% cotton front, back and batting.
The front is hand painted and printed with
fiber reactive dyes. The back is shibori/
immersion dyed also with fiber reactive dyes.

Dyes were applied in a variety of direct
application techniques. The blue fabric was
then hand appliqued and the piece was free
motion quilted in two sections.

Pam RuBert

Springfield, Missouri
USA

I dream of having a designer home like the ones
I see in magazines at the check-out stand of the
grocery store. But in reality, I find that my house is
mysteriously filled with clutter. I'm not sure where it
comes from – maybe the cat has been mail-ordering
stuff again using his cell phone.

43 x 70 inches

Cotton fabrics, cotton and rayon thread,
beads, digital archive prints, photo transfers.

Raw edge applique, machine and hand
stitching.

Dinah Sargeant
Newhall, California
USA

Fledgling
One afternoon my son found a young bird.
Alone and away from the nest, he cradled it, both
struggled.
Through the kitchen window our eyes met and I
watched,
As this boy, now mostly man, considered the
possibilities.

58 x 60 inches

100% cotton fabric hand painted with Rocco
All Fabric paint by the artist, variety of
colored threads, Quilter's Dream cotton
batting.

Hand painted fabric, direct, raw-edge
machine applique, machine quilting.

Joan Schulze
Sunnyvale, California
USA

From my San Francisco studio, I can watch clouds and fog move in and out of the city. The buildings play hide and seek in the fog and changing light strikes reflective surfaces. I am amazed at how many ways I can experience the city from my window. Sunset is often so beautiful all work stops while I soak up the changes.

Pillars is part of an ongoing series of quilts and collages which owes much to my view and how the layers of tall buildings look in the distance. Every window has a story. Hide and Seek is not just a game for children.

43 x 43 inches

Cotton, batting, attached quilt: silk, paper, cotton, metal leaf.

Monoprinting, machine quilting; attached quilt- glue transfer, machine quilting, metal leafing.

Susan Shie

Wooster, Ohio
USA

I started to make this painting about my own life, and then Katrina hit, and the diary I wrote on the painting became her story. Katrina took over my thoughts, like she took over the lives of all those people whose world she turned upside down. And whose world is still turned upside down.

I haven't been down to New Orleans or the coast since Katrina, but they say now, in March, 2006, it looks like it just happened yesterday. We can't forget the hurricanes, the people, the cities, and just let them go to ruin. Please read this quilt's stories as if they'd just happened yesterday, and please tell your congressmen we need to help now, and to please get it right finally. Bring the troops home now, and have them work to restore the Gulf. Please.

45 x 76 inches

Whole cloth painting, cotton fabric, fabric paint, polyfil batting, machine thread, perle cotton embroidery thread, green temple buddha boy bead.

Painting with regular brush, airpen (drawing and writing), machine quilting and small amount of hand quilting.

Katrina Blues

79

Mary Ruth Smith

Waco, Texas

USA

The figure has become a favorite motif in my recent artmaking practices. It amplifies the beauty that can be found in the repetitive nature of the running stitch. Both the figure and the running stitch are used to develop *All in the Family*. Together, they established a way for me to actually make a quilt through layering fabrics and holding them together with stitch. Underlying patches of fabric, colorful threads, and directional changes in stitching provided the ingredients for familial relationships and variations of form.

21 x 21 inches

Hand-dyed fabric, thread.

Dyeing, hand-stitched with running stitch.

Karen N. Soma

Seattle, Washington
USA

Like magma, molten beneath the earth's crust, human
desire, hot with emotion, bubbles up – seeking a
pathway to the surface.

This quilt was inspired by seeing the active volcano
on Hawaii's Big Island. As I looked into the dark
earth and watched the fiery reds and golds of the
lava and its insistent push to the surface, I felt a thrill
of recognition. Here was a metaphor for repressed
desire, for how we can bury our fondest desires
under the structured patterns of our daily lives.
However, those desires can ferment and foment and
push as insistently as lava does to be released and
acknowledged –the fiery essence of who we are.

50 x 32 inches

Pima cotton, Procion MX dyes, fabric
pigments, rayon and metallic threads, beads
and metal findings.

Hand dyeing, screenprinting, shibori,
machine piecing, quilting and embroidery,
fusing, hand beading.

Joan Sowada

Gillette, Wyoming

USA

I choose to take photos of the relationship of people with their environment. At the time of this photo shoot I was so drawn to the shadows, that they became the subject of the photos. Initially I wanted to do this piece because of the exciting repetition of shape and strong graphic design. As I worked on this piece I started to think about the riddle of the elephant and then that became the riddle of the bicycle. If you were not already familiar with a bicycle, what truth could you draw from seeing just one view of a bicycle? When we see a bicycle head on, instead of broadside, it looks like a vertical line! Likewise what can we know of our own experiences when we each have our own perspective. How much can we know of our own world or the universe? *Cosmic Bicycle* is about perspective, the nature of truth, what is known and what is unknown.

35 x 60 inches

Cotton fabrics, (some hand painted and some commercial) 20/80 batting, thread.

Fabrics fused, machine applique and quilting.

Cosmic Bicycle

Connie Tiegel
Atherton, California
USA

Deschutes #1 is a wrapped resist, 100% cotton fabric hand-dyed with Jacquard Procion MX dyes. Simple improvisational cutting, reversing, and sewing of fabric pieces resulted in incredible depth and dimension that reminded me of basalt columns along the Deschutes River. This piece was free motion quilted on a long arm quilting machine to emphasize the dimensional aspects of the piece. The name *Deschutes #1* is in memory of a good day on the beautiful, basalt-columned Deschutes River, Oregon.

81 x 55 inches

100% Pimatex cotton, variegated thread, Warm and Natural batting, Procion MX dyes.

Shibori, machine quilted free motion.

Kristin Tweed

North Fort Myers, Florida
USA

I want to engage the viewer's interest by laying a visual trap.

I use exaggeration to create a spectacle.

The spectacle proclaims the truth about the model's soul.

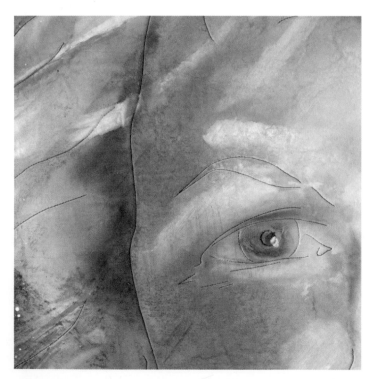

44 x 44 inches

Recycled cotton bed sheets, polyester thread, polyester felt, polyamide fusible web, acrylic thread.

Whole cloth construction, machine quilted, hand painted.

Nelda Warkentin

Anchorage, Alaska
USA

My work is about color, rhythm and pattern found in nature. *Palms Swaying, Whales Breeching* was inspired while visiting Puerto Vallarta, Mexico. The palms danced in the wind and the whales rolled in the waves. The arc, a beautiful line created by each, was simply breathtaking.

50 x 40 inches

Silk, cotton, linen, canvas.

Multiple layers of artist painted silk over cotton and canvas, linen accents.

Barbara W. Watler
Hollywood, Florida
USA

Canadian Sunrise illustrates that magic moment just as the sun begins to rise above the horizon on a still, quiet morning. Trees are backlit with intense colors. The complexity of intertwined trunks and branches creates a network of fascinating intersections which outline shapes that repeat irregularly throughout the composition. These shapes change and evolve in ways that are simultaneously new yet ancient. Similar to working a jigsaw puzzle images unfold with each step of the process but not until completed does this art vibrate with all the positive energy invested in its fabrication.

57 x 57 inches

Cotton blends, bleached muslin backing, Thermore batting, Jacquard textile paint.

Whole cloth reverse applique, machine stitched and embellished, hand painted.

Kathy Weaver

Highland Park, Illinois

USA

My work addresses the intersection between technology and art. By using the labor-intensive quilt medium, nostalgic materials, and the robot persona, the pieces have layers of meaning about time, political conflict and memory.

The robot's setting is that of a tilted stage and in this environment the robot is a translator of events, an alter ego, a doppelganger. The viewer is invited into the picture plane to see the modality of the robot's disposition as it reflects human nature.

Humor, satire, and whimsy add human aspects to the robot. This humor underscores the suspicion that more is afoot than suggested at first glance. Satins and velvets, embroidery and hand sewing, give an intimate touch to the hard-edged, supra natural airbrushed and painted forms. There is an incongruity in the use of soft materials for hard objects and sharp thoughts.

90 x 54 inches

Bridal satin, taffetas, satins, cottons, embroidery floss.

Airbrushed, appliqued, pieced, hand embroidered, hand quilted.

Jill Rumoshosky Werner
Wichita, Kansas
USA

Tangled: Complicated and difficult to unravel.
A messy pile of quilt. The actual quilt is 14 yards
long by 6 inches wide.

28 x 12 x 28 inches

Cotton fabric, stabilizer.

Machine piecing, machine quilting.

Tangled

Elia Woods

Oklahoma City, Oklahoma

USA

What is more beautiful than a lettuce leaf? Closely
examined, a whole world appears. This quilt is a
continuation of my "Vegetable Prayers" series, which
pays visual homage to the splendor of the vegetable
world.

36 x 28 inches

Front of quilt: cotton, photo transfer,
cotton batting, cotton backing.

Photo transfer, machine pieced, machine
quilted.

Artists & Quilts Index